Business as

a Baby

Nurturing your Business from Infancy to Success

Library of Congress Control Number: 2024952530

ISBN: 978-978-773-205-2(Paperback)
ISBN: 978-978-773-204-5 (Hardcover)
ISBN: 978-978-771-951-0 (Ebook)
ISBN: 978-978-773-206-9(Audio Book)

Author by Chukwudum "Chumze" Chukwudebelu
Book Cover Design by Nimi Diffa.
Book Style and Guide by Nmerichukwu Igweammaka
Co - Editor by Dr. Chinyere Julie Chukwudebelu
Co - Editor by Kent Alexander Thachek

Printed by TheChumEffect, LLC., in the United States of America.

First printing edition 2024.

TheChumEffect, LLC
2025 Guadalupe Street, Ste 260
Austin Texas, 78705

https://thechumeffect.com/

Business as a Baby

Table of Contents.

Business as a Baby

Preface

Summary

In the world of entrepreneurship, we often hear stories of overnight successes and rapid growth. But the reality of building a business is far more nuanced, challenging, and, in many ways, beautiful. This book, "Business as a Baby," is born from my own journey of triumphs and tribulations, and the profound lessons I learned along the way.

My entrepreneurial path began with a simple idea: an app called Chumz that would revolutionize the college textbook market. Fueled by ambition and armed with my computer engineering degree, I dove headfirst into the world of startups. However, like many first-time entrepreneurs, I made the critical mistake of treating my fledgling venture like an established corporation. The result? A painful but invaluable lesson in humility and the true nature of building a business.

The failure of Chumz led me to a period of deep introspective reflection. During this time, I began to see the parallels between raising a child and nurturing a business. Both require patience, constant attention, and the understanding that growth happens in stages. You would not expect a baby to run before it could crawl, so why do we often expect our businesses to sprint before they can walk?

This realization gave birth to the Business as a Baby (BAAB) framework. It is a methodical approach that guides entrepreneurs through the growth stages of their ventures, emphasizing patience, adaptability, and realistic expectations. Armed with this new perspective, I applied these principles to my consulting firm, TheChumEffect (TCE), and saw a transformative change in both the business's growth and my own approach to entrepreneurship.

The BAAB framework is not just theory – it is a practical, tested approach. One of my clients, Valentine Nwachukwu, the CEO/Founder of Zaden technologies Inc, applied these principles to his teenage company with remarkable results. The framework added significant value to his business, helping him navigate challenges and foster sustainable growth. It was Valentine who, seeing the transformative impact of BAAB on his own company, strongly encouraged me to write this book. He recognized that these insights could help countless other entrepreneurs facing similar challenges. Valentine's enthusiasm and the tangible results he achieved were the final push I needed to share these concepts with a broader audience.

"Business as a Baby" is thus not just my story, but a testament to the real-world applicability of the BAAB framework. It is a collection of insights drawn from my own experiences, the successful application in my consulting firm TheChumEffect (TCE), and the positive outcomes achieved by clients like Zaden Technologies. This book is as much a result of their successes and encouragement as it is of my own journey.

Whether you are a first-time founder, a seasoned entrepreneur, an established company launching a new division, a consulting firm guiding clients, a small business owner expanding into new markets, an innovation team within a large organization, or someone nurturing a side hustle, this book offers a fresh perspective on business growth. It is about learning to love the process, understanding the natural stages of business development, and giving your venture the care and attention it needs to thrive.

As you read this book, I encourage you to reflect on your own journey. Embrace the baby steps, celebrate the small victories, and remember that every successful business you admire today once started as someone's baby idea.

This book is more than just a guide to starting a business. It is a call to change how we think about entrepreneurship. It is an invitation to embrace the messy, unpredictable, and often chaotic journey of building something from nothing. Through each chapter, you will find insights drawn from real experiences, strategies that have been tested in the crucible of actual business challenges, and a perspective that I hope will fundamentally shift how you approach your entrepreneurial journey.

Welcome to "Business as a Baby." Let us nurture some ideas into reality.

Chukwudum "Chumze" Chukwudebelu
CEO/Founder of TheChumEffect (TCE)
Creator of the Business as a Baby (BAAB) Framework.

Introduction

A Journey from Textbooks to Tech: My Entrepreneurial Tale

The Beginnings of a Young Entrepreneur

Once upon a time, in the not-so-distant past, there was a young graduate in his early twenties, fresh-faced and eager to make his mark on the world. Having recently donned the cap and gown, I emerged from college with a bachelor's degree in computer engineering tucked under my arm, a symbol of my academic achievements and a passport to my future endeavors. But my story begins with a different kind of education—the entrepreneurial kind. You see, even before I could proudly frame my degree, I had dabbled in the art of commerce. I had found a niche in the bustling marketplace of books. My business was simple yet ingenious: I would scour the internet for used textbooks, snapping them up at bargain prices, and then I would play the matchmaker, pairing these books with bookstores willing to pay a premium. Often, they fetched twice or sometimes even thrice what I had paid.

The Young Businessman at Work

I still recall the picture of my mother, her eyes filled with a mix of pride and curiosity, as she watched me pack a box of books for shipment. Every fortnight, like clockwork, I would send off my literary troves and in return, $2000 would find its way into my bank account. This venture, which had taken root in my junior year of college, was not just profitable—it was a promise of what I could achieve.

A Dream Takes Flight

As the days of college became cherished memories, I stood at a crossroads. The entrepreneur within me was restless, yearning for more than just a transactional affair with books. It was time to scale, to evolve, to dream bigger. And so, with the fire of ambition fueling my resolve, I set out to transform my fledgling enterprise. The vision was clear: an app that could automate my entire business process. From this fervent desire, the chumz app, and its accompanying company, was born.

Lessons in Patience

But the life of an entrepreneur is never without its trials and tribulations. I managed chumz with the seriousness and dedication one would expect of a Fortune 500 company, but alas, my creation was still in its infancy. It needed nurturing, not the heavy hand of a seasoned conglomerate. In my impatience, I made hasty decisions, ones that led to the app's untimely demise. Two years of introspection followed—a period of internal struggle where I sought to pin the blame on vendors, on software—but the truth was far simpler and harder to accept. I had rushed the infant company, trying to launch at multiple schools simultaneously without first securing its ability to survive and thrive.

From Ashes to Insight

It was a painful realization, seeing that my impatience had been the architect of my downfall. I had dreamed of dominating the market as if chumz was a full-grown enterprise, but it was merely a child in the vast playground of business. It was this epiphany that gave birth to the Business as a Baby (BAAB) framework—a step-by-step process that guides entrepreneurs through the growth stages of their venture. It teaches patience, foresight, and the art of decision-making.

The Cycle of Business Life

And so, this narrative brings us to the present and to the introduction of my book, "Business as Baby (BAAB)." It is a testament to the journey that every towering corporate once began as a fragile start-up, a baby in the world of commerce. We must view these fledgling companies through the lens of growth stages—from Baby to Toddler, to Teenager, and finally to adult.

It stands as a gentle reminder to all who dare to dream and create: What stage do you believe your business is in? Are you nurturing it according to its needs, allowing it to grow and mature at its own pace? The BAAB framework is not just a method; it is the story of my own growth as an entrepreneur, a guide meant to steer your company through the tumultuous but rewarding journey from inception to maturity.

Chapter 1

How to View Your Business as a Baby

The purpose of viewing your business as a baby is to understand that your business is a separate entity from you. This differentiation makes it easier to draw boundaries and protect the "baby" from its "parents," who might mistakenly think they are the business.

When you view your business as a baby, you recognize that it is a separate entity requiring significant attention, much like a newborn. Let us consider this analogy: when raising a newborn, the baby stays up all night, cries, and focuses solely on eating, sleeping, and bodily functions.

While caring for a baby that cannot communicate its needs, you must rely on instinct to sense and fulfill their basic survival requirements. There is no structure to this process—it is all intuition. When a baby cries, you instinctively check to see if they need sleep, food, or a diaper change.

The reason for viewing your business through this lens is that many entrepreneurs try to approach it from an overly structured perspective. When expecting a baby (or starting a business), parents often get excited and make elaborate plans—buying cribs, clothes, and shoes. However, babies grow quickly, and businesses must iterate rapidly. Just as babies outgrow things fast, your business will need to adapt continuously.

Consider this example:

An entrepreneur wanted to start a company and had grandiose plans. Before acquiring any customers, they recruited an executive, believing it was a great idea. However, they viewed the business as something to be managed rather than nurtured—two hugely different approaches. At this stage, they were not making instinctive decisions. They assumed their customers would come from a certain market based on research, but when they launched, they had to close the business because they had spent too much of their raised capital. Instead of instinctively understanding what the "baby" business needed at that point, they placed too many expectations on it, leading to its demise.

You must find a way to view your business like a baby, recognizing that everything takes small steps. Once you simplify from this perspective, it becomes easier to develop your business.

Another common mistake is when first-time entrepreneurs quit their jobs to embark on the journey of business ownership, inspired by romanticized portrayals in movies. However, this raises important questions: How will you feed the "baby" during this period? What is your plan for covering necessities like housing and food for yourself while caring for your business? This scenario happens often—people have not even gotten their business to survive, yet they are trying to rely on a "baby" that needs them to live.

Consider this: When parents have a newborn, do they quit their jobs? No, they typically take parental leave, during which they receive pay or use savings. They do not expect the baby to support them someday; they understand that the baby needs their care, love, and attention to survive.

A nascent business needs similar nurturing. All the sleepless nights and stress are part of the process, and you must lower your expectations, remembering that this is a "baby."

Here is another example to illustrate this point:

Imagine you want to start a real estate company and buy properties. Let us assume that you are earning $50,000 per year with excellent credit, but you are focused on starting with a property that requires a $20,000 down payment—which would take about four years to save. The problem is that you are not thinking from a "baby" perspective. You are not considering how you could get a property with zero down payment at your current income level and convert it to an investment property

20

later. This scenario is more conducive to the state of your finances as well.

If you viewed it like a baby, you would calculate your current rent, see if you can find a property with zero down, and start from there. Build up gradually, make improvements. Perhaps develop it into a dwelling for yourself so that you can stop paying rent in the long term. Then sell the property once it is fully developed, using that money to further finance the purchase of other assets or developments.

Methods like this are known as house hacking, where you live in one part of the property and rent out others, or using existing home equity through refinancing, can also be used to enter real estate with minimal or no down payment. You are viewing it like a baby in this sense, you remove unnecessary pressure and put yourself in a position where you are not forced to rush the business's growth, which often leads to failure and giving up.

There might be other opportunities to consider that would boost the baby real estate business growth. More specifically, you could enter a joint venture, where you acquire property suitable for development, and then partner with an experienced developer. Together, you would agree on profit sharing, roles, and capital contributions, where your role might focus on financial management and initial acquisition, while the developer handles the development process.

You can even lease the land to commercial and residential developers, depending on where it is and how you acquired the property. After development, the property's profits from sales or leases are split as per the agreement. This setup allows you to mitigate financial risk as well by sharing part of it with the developer, but still requires careful planning, legal structuring, and market understanding to ensure success.

Consider the uncertainties of the future: What if other life events occur in five years, such as marriage or having children? If you viewed the baby as an adult prematurely, you may have put the business under too much pressure and never even brought it to life. You must consistently view it as a baby, taking small, manageable steps.

When you view your business as a baby, it reinforces the idea that you need to take simple steps. Be gentle with it so it can develop accordingly, and do not burden yourself with false expectations that this "baby" is supposed to take care of you right away.

Reflective Questions

1. *In what ways are you currently treating your business like an adult rather than a baby? How might this be hindering its growth?*

2. *What unrealistic expectations have you set for your business? How can you adjust these to be more appropriate for its current stage?*

3. *How can you create a more nurturing environment for your baby business? What specific changes in your approach or mindset are needed?*

4. *Reflect on a recent business decision. How might that decision have been different if you had approached it with a "baby business" mindset?*

5. *What small, manageable steps can you take in the next month to align your business practices with the "baby business" concept?*

Chapter 2

Understanding the Baby Business: It is All About Survival

The Raw Reality of a Baby Business

Let us get one thing straight: a baby business is just that - a baby. It is not a miniature version of a big corporation. It is a fragile, newborn venture that is just trying to survive. When you are running a baby business, you are not thinking about growth strategies, market dominance, or fancy business models. You are thinking about making it through another day, another week, another month.

Understanding Through Real Baby Examples

To truly grasp what it means to run a baby business, let us look at actual babies:

The 2-Year-Old Mess Maker

Imagine you have a 2-year-old child. This kid is going to make messes. They will throw food, spill drinks, and create chaos. As a parent, what do you do? You clean up after them patiently. You do not yell at them for not using a fork properly or for spilling their juice. Why? Because you understand they are still learning.

Now, apply this to your baby business. It is going to make messes. It is going to have days where everything seems to go wrong. Your job is not to get frustrated or to expect perfection. It is to clean up the messes, learn from them, and keep moving forward.

The 1-Year-Old Learning to Walk

Now think about a 1-year-old learning to walk. They are going to fall. A lot. They will stumble, crawl, pull themselves up on furniture, and fall again. Do you see anyone trying to give them crutches or a wheelchair? Of course not. You let them fall, you encourage them to get back up, and you celebrate every wobbly step.

This is exactly how you need to treat your baby business. It is learning to walk in the business world. It is going to stumble and fall. Your job is to let it fall safely, encourage it to get back up, and celebrate every small victory.

Forget What You Think You Know

Here is the first thing you need to understand: throw out everything you have read in those shiny business books or heard from so-called experts about running a "successful business." Most of that does not apply to you. At least not yet. Why? Because those strategies and tactics are for grown-up businesses. You are dealing with a newborn here. This is akin to the fact that a baby can neither run nor walk, let alone stand on their own two feet. Your baby business will surely get there, but only if it can survive, which is precisely why this notion cannot be emphasized enough.

The Only Goal: Survival

Your only goal right now is to survive. That is all! Do not let anyone tell you otherwise. You are not here to disrupt markets, scale rapidly, or become the next unicorn. You are here to keep your baby business alive long enough for it to learn how to crawl, then walk, then maybe someday run.

The Comparison Trap

One of the biggest mistakes you can make is comparing your baby business to established companies. It is like comparing a toddler to a full-grown adult. It does not make sense, and it is only going to mess with your head. Let us look at how this works in practice, using video streaming services as an example.

The Netflix Trap

Say you want to launch a video streaming platform. It is tempting to look at Netflix and think, "That's what success looks like. I need to be like them." But let us get real for a second. Netflix is a giant. They have:

- Billions of dollars to throw around
- A massive library of content
- Deals with major studios
- Millions of subscribers worldwide
- Teams of developers working on their platform

You, as a baby streaming business, have none of that. And that is okay. Netflix did not start out with all that either. They also started out as a baby business, however, first offering movie rentals through a mail-order system. Netflix launched in 1997 with a model where customers could rent DVDs online and have them mailed to their homes. This was innovative because it eliminated late fees and offered a vast selection. Netflix later transitioned into streaming 10 years later, long after they had established themselves. At a certain point, the ability to re-invest in their company and completely change the underlying operational business model became feasible. Therefore, a baby has no business in considering these developments until they have passed the stage of infancy.

What you should not do:

- Try to compete with Netflix's content library
- Aim for millions of subscribers right away
- Spend money you do not have on flashy original productions

What you should do:

- Focus on a specific niche that bigger platforms might be overlooking
- Maybe partner with local content creators or indie filmmakers
- Start small, even in just one city or region
- Learn what your small audience likes and build from there

Remember, Netflix started by mailing DVDs to people, which was extremely simple. They did not jump straight into streaming, let alone producing their own original content. They grew into that over time.

Your job is not to be the next Netflix. Your job is to be the best baby streaming service you can be right now. Focus on surviving, learning, and slowly growing your audience.

The Power of Being Small and Unknown

Here is something most people will not tell you: being small and unknown is a superpower. Why? Because you can mess up, and nobody cares. Just like that 2-year-old making a mess at home, you can try things, fail, and try again without ending up in the news or disappointing shareholders.

Use this to your advantage. Try things. Fail. Learn. Repeat. This is your time to figure out what works and what does not without the world watching.

Real-World Examples

Let us explore further using practical examples:

The Restaurant Dream

Say you want to open a restaurant. The "grown-up" approach would be to get a big loan, rent a fancy space, hire a full staff, and launch with a big grand opening.

31

That is the quickest way to kill your baby business before it even starts walking.

Instead, think like a baby business:

- Start with one great dish you know how to make.
- Sell it from your home kitchen or a food truck.
- Learn what people like and do not like.
- Slowly add more dishes as you figure things out.

You are not trying to be a five-star restaurant right out of the gate. You are just trying to survive and learn.

The Tech Startup Fantasy

Everyone wants to be the next big tech company. But if you are a baby business, forget about competing with the giants. You do not need a fancy office, a team of developers, or millions in venture capital.

Start small:

- Build one simple feature that solves one specific problem.

- Find a handful of people who really need that solution.
- Learn from them. Improve based on their feedback.
- Grow slowly, one user at a time if you must.

You are not aiming to be the next Facebook. You are aiming to still be in business next month.

The Hard Truth About Resources

Here is something you need to accept you do not have resources. You are going to be doing everything on a shoestring budget, probably while still working another job to pay your bills. That is the reality of a baby business.

You cannot afford fancy tools, big marketing campaigns, or a team of experts. And you should not be thinking about those things anyway. Your resources are your time, your energy, and a little bit of savings. Use them wisely, just like you would carefully manage your time and energy with a real baby.

The Myth of the Overnight Success

Let us bust a myth right now: there is no such thing as an overnight success. Every business you admire started as a baby, just like yours. They struggled, they made mistakes, and they barely survived their early days.

The difference is, they kept at it. They survived long enough to grow up. That is your job right now - survive long enough to grow up. Just like you would not expect a 1-year-old to suddenly start running marathons, do not expect your baby business to suddenly compete with industry giants.

Embracing the Baby Business Mindset

Understanding that you are running a baby business is liberating. It means:

- You do not need to have all the answers.
- It is okay to start small and messy.
- Learning is more important than perfection.
- Survival is success at this stage.

Conclusion: Stay Alive, Keep Learning

Running a baby business is not about grand strategies or rapid growth. It is about staying alive and learning every single day. Every day your business survives is a success. Every mistake is a lesson.

Do not let anyone pressure you into thinking you need to be bigger, faster, or more successful right away. Your job is to nurture your baby business, help it learn to walk, and give it the chance to grow up. Just like you would not rush a child's development, do not rush your business's growth.

Remember, every big business started as a baby. Your time will come. For now, focus on survival. Everything else can wait. Embrace the messy, wobbly, sometimes frustrating journey of raising your baby business. It is the only way it will ever have a chance to grow into something great.

Reflective Questions

1. *How are you currently viewing your business? As a baby that needs nurturing, or as something more advanced. How might shifting your perspective change your approach?*

2. *What "messes" has your baby business made recently? How did you handle them, and what did you learn from the experience?*

3. *In what ways might you be setting unrealistic expectations for your business based on comparisons to established companies? How can you adjust these expectations?*

4. *Considering the "Netflix Trap" example, what specific niche or underserved market*

could your business focus on instead of trying to compete with industry giants?

5. *How do you leverage your "superpower" of being small and unknown in your current business operations?*

Chapter 3

Patience When Raising a Baby Business

Understanding Patience

Patience is more than the ability to wait for something to occur. It is a complex skill that requires inner stillness and vision. Consider this poem I wrote about patience:

Good things come to those who wait.
Be still and do not get ill.
Feel the air close to you.
Absorb the knowledge around you.
Exercise patience literally.
Mind the thoughts you have.
Give back to yourself.
In time everything will connect.

Take a moment to let these words simmer in your soul before we delve deeper into the concept of patience and its crucial role in nurturing a baby business.

The Challenge of Patience

Being patient is not an easy task. It requires you to:

- Sit tight and live in the vision while waiting for something to happen.
- Tune out the present moment and live in the future of what you are waiting for.
- Understand that everything needs time to grow or reach its potential.
- Have an innate belief in what you are envisioning for the future.

Patience is an underrated skill, yet it is essential for success in business and life.

Another perspective on patience is the ability to give what you are being patient with time to catch up with your vision. It is about allowing your expectations to align with reality, giving your goals time to materialize without destroying the natural rhythm with premature or unrealistic expectations.

Patience with a Baby Business

Approaching your business as if it is a baby requires significant sacrifice, endurance, and emotional investment. You must simultaneously hold the vision of what your business will become while avoiding the pitfall of imposing futuristic expectations on it in its current state. Like a real baby, your business lacks the ability to understand or meet advanced expectations at once.

Consider this example: If a six-month-old baby is making a mess, you would not scold them or expect them to understand complex instructions. You clean up after them because you recognize their limitations. Similarly, you would not shout at a baby for wetting their diaper. Your awareness that you are dealing with a baby makes it easier to approach the situation with patience.

Many entrepreneurs, however, are impatient with their baby businesses. They try to manage them like mature enterprises, communicating as if the business has adult-level understanding. This approach does not recognize that, like babies, new businesses are experiencing the world for the first time. Even if the founder is not new to entrepreneurship, each business venture is novel and requires a fresh, patient approach.

The Perils of Impatience: A Personal Example

I experienced the consequences of impatience firsthand when launching my book app. I was fixated on launching during the school year when book sales typically peak. However, I forgot a crucial fact: my business was still in its infancy. There would be time for growth, but survival was the primary goal at that stage.

This impatience led to rash decisions that contributed to the demise of that baby business. It is a stark reminder that not every baby business will survive, just as not every startup succeeds. Sometimes, the environment is too harsh, or the business is not built to withstand certain pressures. In some cases, a baby business might evolve into a hobby rather than a full-fledged enterprise, and that is okay.

The Virtue of Patience in Business Growth

Patience truly is a virtue, especially when nurturing a baby business. Here are some scenarios where impatience can be detrimental:

- In sports, many hyped prospects fade away due to impatience and excessive pressure. Not every talent is built to survive intense scrutiny from the start.

- Large companies often launch new ventures (baby businesses) and fail because they try to scale too quickly, treating them like established products.

- Consider the case of Google Meet versus Zoom. Google Meet, despite coming out before Zoom, struggled because Google treated it like an adult product, using its existing user base and resources. They assumed customers would adopt it simply because they used other Google products. In contrast, Zoom focused on customer needs and capitalized on the COVID-19 pandemic, propelling them to success.

This is why you often see large companies or private equity firms buy startups and give them autonomy. They recognize the value of nurturing these baby businesses while learning from their innovative approaches.

The Importance of Customer Feedback

Being patient with a baby business also means being open to customer feedback and willing to adapt. Google's experience with Google Hangouts (which could have rivaled WhatsApp or Facebook Messenger) illustrates this point. If they had approached Hangouts like a baby business and listened to customer needs— such as allowing sign-ups with phone numbers or integrating with other email providers—they might have gained a significant market share. Instead, their impatience and assumption that their existing resources and user base were sufficient, is what led to WhatsApp dominating the smartphone chat market.

A key aspect where Google could have benefited from treating Hangouts like a baby business was in listening to and acting upon customer feedback. For instance, the lack of easy sign-up using phone numbers, unlike WhatsApp's straightforward approach, limited

Hangouts' appeal. Moreover, its deep integration with Google services made it less accessible to users outside the Google ecosystem, a critical oversight in capturing the casual, cross-platform user base that WhatsApp successfully attracted.

The consequence of these strategic decisions was that Google Hangouts did not gain the widespread adoption necessary to compete with WhatsApp, which by leveraging simplicity, cross-platform availability, and focusing on international markets, became a dominant player in mobile messaging. Google's later attempts to rectify this with services like Google Allo or pushing for RCS messaging have not managed to regain the lost ground, proving how initial impatience and lack of adaptability can cost significant market share in tech sectors where timing and user experience are everything.

Conclusion: Patience as a Must-Have Virtue

At the end of the day, being patient with a baby business is crucial for its survival. Avoid putting your business under unnecessary pressure or imposing unrealistic expectations. Remember that having substantial resources does not guarantee success—in fact, it can lead to "superhuman stupidity," enabling rash decisions that might seem feasible but eventually harm the business.

Patience is indeed a virtue, but patience with a baby business is an absolute necessity. You cannot learn, grow, or succeed without it. As you nurture your baby business, remember to give it time, listen to your customers, and allow it to develop at its own pace. With patience and perseverance, you will be better equipped to guide your business from infancy to maturity, avoiding the pitfalls that come with premature expectations and rushed growth.

Reflective Questions

1. *Are you spending too much time dreaming about future success? How can you refocus on present survival?*

2. *In which areas of your business do you find it most challenging to be patient? Why do you think these areas are particularly difficult?*

3. *How has impatience affected your business decisions in the past? What were the outcomes, and what did you learn?*

4. *What strategies can you implement to cultivate more patience in your day-to-day business operations?*

5. *Reflect on a time when patience paid off in your business. How can you apply the lessons from that experience to your current challenges?*

6. *How can you reframe your long-term goals into smaller, more manageable milestones that require patience to achieve?*

Chapter 4

The Future is Only Survival for a Baby Business

The Present Reality of a Baby Business

There is a saying that the past is a delusion, and the future is an illusion—only the present is real. This wisdom is particularly relevant when it comes to nurturing a baby business. Too often, entrepreneurs spend excessive time thinking about the future of their venture, daydreaming about the good days when the business will be mature and self-sustaining. This future-focused mindset can lead to detrimental decisions and unrealistic expectations.

The Danger of Future-Focused Thinking

When you are overly focused on the future, you risk:

- Starving yourself and indirectly hurting your baby business
- Putting the business in a position to make decisions it is not equipped to handle
- Forgetting that the business has not yet survived its crucial early stages

The only future that should exist for a baby business is the immediate one: "How can this baby survive today, tomorrow, and the day after?" It is only after the baby has survived that you can worry about growth.

Survival Before Growth

Many entrepreneurs worry prematurely about issues like intellectual property (IP) or competition from established companies. However, just as adults do not typically bully infants, established businesses are unlikely to see your baby business as a threat. You have not even survived long enough to prove that there is an opportunity in your chosen market.

The only future you should be concerned with is survival. Everything else—growth, competition, expansion—comes after you have ensured your business can consistently stay afloat.

A Personal Example:

The Chumz App

Let me share a personal example from my entrepreneurial journey. After college, I launched an e-commerce book platform called the Chumz app—a marketplace for college students to resell their textbooks directly to each other. I made the mistake of worrying about unrealistic futures:

- I thought about launching on multiple college campuses simultaneously
- I assembled a team, wrote a business plan, and shared equity
- I worried about competitors like Chegg stealing my idea

What I should have focused on was launching the product and getting actual users, even if it was only from one department for a single semester. The survival of a baby business is in the hands of its customers, not in grand plans or fears of competition.

The Fallacy of Funding as Survival

Do not fall into the trap of thinking that raising money for your startup equates to survival, especially without customers. This false sense of accomplishment can lead to:

- Superhuman stupidity and misplaced wisdom
- A false aura of invincibility
- Forgetting that a business survives on consistent income from paying customers, not investors

Investor money still needs to be returned with interest. Often, investors put the baby business under immense pressure before it has achieved a stable customer base, leading to premature failure. Remember, 9 out of 10 startups fail—focusing on glossy futures instead of day-to-day survival is a common mistake.

The AI Example: A Baby Industry

Consider the current state of Artificial Intelligence (AI). Many established companies are investing heavily in the AI ecosystem, thinking far into the future. However, the industry is still in its infancy, and the ecosystem is not mature enough for an adult version to thrive.

This situation is reminiscent of the dot-com era during the early adoption of the internet:

- Companies invested heavily in internet services and technology
- Mass adoption had not occurred yet
- The ecosystem (high-speed internet, smartphones, etc.) was not fully developed

It was not until the ecosystem matured—with the advent of smartphones, advanced semiconductors, and widespread high-speed internet—that companies like Amazon could truly take off. The same process is likely to occur with AI as the ecosystem develops, including an increase in skilled AI workers and advances in computing power like quantum computers.

The Perils of Premature Commitment

Another classic mistake is when a founder quits their day job for a baby business that has not yet survived. This puts unnecessary pressure on both the founder and the business because:

- You are living in an imagined future
- You make bad decisions due to financial stress
- You expect a baby business to support an adult lifestyle

Remember, babies cannot take care of parents—they do not have the ability. Expecting your baby business to immediately replace your job is like yelling at an infant for not turning off the lights to save on the electricity bill.

Focus on Present-Day Survival

Every decision for a baby business should be about present-day survival. Ask yourself:

- What does the business need to survive today?
- What small, achievable steps can I take right now?

It is okay to dream about your vision, but when executing, focus on immediate survival rather than long-term goals that may put undue pressure on your fledgling venture.

The Pitfalls of Premature Scaling

Many startups raise seed funding and immediately start running like established companies—hiring aggressively, lacking flexibility, and burning through cash without sustainable income. This approach often leads to:

- Unsustainable cash flow
- Pressure to continually raise more funding
- Dilution of ownership and loss of control
- Inability to pivot when necessary

The Importance of Flexibility

Remember that the adult business you envision may evolve into something different. Just as a parent's vision of their child becoming a doctor might change when the child decides to become a lawyer, your business may pivot as it grows. Flexibility is key to survival. Amazon, for example, started as an online bookstore but pivoted to become a general e-commerce platform and then expanded into cloud computing with Amazon Web Service (AWS). If they had rigidly stuck to their original vision, they might not have survived and thrived as they have.

The idea that an adult business might evolve significantly from its initial concept is well-illustrated by Amazon's journey. Originally launched in 1994 as an online bookstore, Amazon's founder Jeff Bezos envisioned a vast digital library. However, recognizing the potential in broader e-commerce, Amazon expanded into selling various products by the late '90s, beyond just books was critical for its survival during the dotcom bust.

Flexibility is what allowed Amazon to pivot entirely into new domains. In 2006, AWS was launched, entering, and eventually dominating the cloud computing market. Quite the feat, in and of itself. If Amazon had rigidly adhered to its original bookstore model, it might not have achieved its status as a global commerce and tech leader, showing how adaptability can lead to unexpected avenues of growth and success.

Notice how the lesson here is clear: businesses need to be prepared to adapt alongside market changes, technological advancements, or shifts in consumer behavior. Like a child choosing a different career path than what was expected, a business must be flexible enough to pivot, when necessary, as rigidity can lead to missed opportunities or failure in a constantly evolving market landscape. As such, a baby business must always keep this forward-thinking mindset imbued within its company culture.

Conclusion: Focus on the Present, Survive for the Future

In nurturing a baby business, rigidity will only get you through obstacles you overcome. Flexibility, on the other hand, allows you to adapt to any obstacle because you can take different forms depending on the challenge in front of you.

This is how you survive with a baby business in the present—by morphing your way to that future. Only after your baby has survived does the real journey begin. Do not get trapped by the illusions of the future, forgetting that the only real thing for your baby business is the present. Focus on survival today, and you will build a foundation for success tomorrow.

Reflective Questions

1. *How much of your time and energy are currently focused on your future plans versus your present survival? How can you shift this balance?*

2. *What immediate survival need is your business facing right now? How can you address these more effectively?*

3. *In what ways might you be putting unnecessary pressure on your baby business to perform like a mature company? How can you alleviate this pressure?*

4. *What is the best way to separate your personal financial needs from your business's current capabilities? What adjustments might be necessary?*

5. *What small, achievable steps can you take right now to ensure your business's survival in the next month? The next quarter?*

Chapter 5

Endurance in Raising Your Baby Business

Understanding Endurance in Entrepreneurship

Endurance, in the context of raising a baby business, is more than just perseverance. It is the ability to bear an infinite amount of pressure, stress, and responsibility while continuing to move forward. This quality is essential for entrepreneurs because the journey of nurturing a startup is fraught with challenges, setbacks, and unexpected turns.

The Multifaceted Nature of Entrepreneurial Endurance

- Emotional Endurance: Dealing with the highs and lows of business without losing your mental equilibrium.
- Physical Endurance: Maintaining your health and energy levels despite long hours and high stress.
- Financial Endurance: Managing resources carefully and weathering periods of financial uncertainty.
- Strategic Endurance: Staying committed to your long-term vision while remaining flexible in your approach.

The Emotional Rollercoaster of a Baby Business

As you nurture your fledgling venture, you will often find yourself on an emotional rollercoaster, experiencing a wide range of feelings, sometimes simultaneously:

- Excitement about future success

- Fear of potential failure
- Pride in small achievements
- Frustration with slow progress
- Anxiety about financial stability
- Joy in creative problem-solving

These contradictory emotions can create a tumultuous internal landscape. Learning to manage these emotional whirlwinds is crucial because if it overwhelms you, it can negatively impact your decision-making and overall well-being.

Case Study: The Emotional Journey of a Tech Startup Founder

Consider the story of Sarah, a software engineer who left her stable job to launch a tech startup. In the first month alone, she experienced:

- Elation when securing her first investor meeting
- Disappointment when that investor passed on the opportunity
- Excitement when completing the first working prototype

- Anxiety when realizing the prototype had major flaws
- Pride when hiring her first employee
- Fear when contemplating making payroll

Sarah's ability to navigate these emotional swings without losing sight of her goals was key to her eventual success.

The Danger of Emotional Overidentification

A common pitfall for entrepreneurs is allowing their identity to become too closely intertwined with their baby business. This overidentification can lead to:

- Poor decision-making based on emotional rather than rational factors
- Neglect of self-care, leading to burnout
- Psychological stress that bleeds into personal relationships
- Difficulty in objectively evaluating business performance

To avoid these issues, it is essential to maintain a level of emotional detachment. Recognize that you are raising a baby business, but you are not the business itself. This perspective allows you to process emotions effectively and make better decisions.

Techniques for Maintaining Emotional Distance

- **Regular self-reflection:** Set aside time each week to examine your emotional state and its impact on your decision-making.
- **Mindfulness practices:** Incorporate meditation or other mindfulness techniques to stay grounded in the present.
- **Seeking outside perspectives:** Regularly consult mentors, advisors, or peer groups for objective feedback.
- **Clear work-life boundaries:** Establish and maintain clear boundaries between your work and personal life.

The Illusion of Future Scenarios

A lot of the emotions you experience during this phase stem from anticipating futures that do not yet exist. You might find yourself:

- Dreaming of spectacular success: IPOs, industry awards, media recognition

- Fearing catastrophic failure: bankruptcy, public embarrassment, loss of investment

However, it is crucial to remember that these scenarios are illusions. They do not exist in the present moment and fixating on them can distract you from the immediate needs of your baby business.

The Danger of Future-Focused Thinking

When you are overly focused on the future, you risk:

- Neglecting present-day operations and opportunities
- Making decisions based on imagined scenarios rather than current realities
- Overlooking small but considerable progress in favor of grand future visions
- Becoming paralyzed by fear of potential future failures

Being fixated with future possibilities can pose several dangers to business development. When leaders or entrepreneurs become too absorbed with what might happen down the line, they often neglect the immediate needs and opportunities of their current operations. This can lead to missed chances for growth, as the present is where actionable steps can be taken to build a stronger foundation. Additionally, decision-making can become speculative when it is based more on hypothetical future scenarios, rather than grounded in the tangible realities of today. This might result in strategies that are not feasible or relevant.

A mindset that is overly focused on the future tends to undervalue incremental progress, where small wins and daily improvements are crucial for long-term success. Instead, there is an overemphasis on some grand vision or pie-in-the-sky that might never materialize as envisioned. Moreover, this constant concern for future outcomes can foster a fear of failure, causing paralysis in making key decisions or taking calculated risks today, which could otherwise lead to growth or necessary adoption.

Staying Grounded in the Present

Instead of getting lost in these imaginary futures, focus on the immediate needs of your baby business:

1. Business Fundamentals:

- Completing necessary registrations and legal requirements
- Setting up basic financial systems and tracking
- Establishing a simple but professional online presence

2. Customer Acquisition and Understanding:

- Finding and reaching out to potential first customers
- Conducting in-depth interviews with early adopters
- Analyzing feedback and usage patterns

3. Product or Service Refinement:

- Iterating on your offering based on real user feedback
- Focusing on solving core problems effectively before adding features
- Streamlining operations to deliver value efficiently

4. Building Relationships:

- Networking within your industry
- Forming partnerships with complementary businesses
- Cultivating relationships with mentors and advisors

By focusing on these present-day activities, you create a solid foundation for future growth while avoiding the pitfalls of excessive future-oriented thinking.

The Endurance Phase: Navigating Highs and Lows

The endurance phase of your baby business is characterized by emotional highs and lows. This period is one of the few aspects you can control, as it depends on your temperament and how you react to various situations.

Strategies for Emotional Regulation

- **Celebrate small wins:** Acknowledge and appreciate minor achievements to maintain motivation.
- **Learn from setbacks:** View failures as learning opportunities rather than devastating blows.
- **Maintain perspective:** Regularly remind yourself of your long-term goals and the temporary nature of current challenges.
- **Practice self-care:** Prioritize your physical and mental health through regular exercise, adequate sleep, and stress-management techniques.
- **Build a support network:** Surround yourself with understanding friends, family, and fellow entrepreneurs who can offer emotional support.

From Theory to Practice: The Reality Check

When you first conceive a business idea, you typically start with theoretical planning:

- Extensive market research
- Detailed sales strategies
- Complex financial projections
- Ambitious growth plans

During this phase, it is easy to get caught up in the excitement of potential future success. However, when you move to practical execution, reality sets in, and you may experience anxiety or doubt.

The Theoretical vs. Practical Gap

Theoretical Planning	Practical Reality
Smooth growth curves	Unpredictable fluctuations
Ideal customer personas	Diverse and complex real customers
Perfect product-market fit	Constant tweaking and pivoting
Linear progress	Two steps forward, one step back

Learning to bridge this gap between theory and practice is a crucial skill for entrepreneurs. It requires flexibility, resilience, and a willingness to adapt your plans based on real-world feedback.

Case Study: The Drop Shipping Business

To illustrate the challenges of endurance in entrepreneurship, let us consider an entrepreneur starting a drop shipping business:

- They meticulously research their product niche
- Set up relationships with suppliers on AliExpress
- Create a visually appealing Shopify store
- Launch with a carefully planned marketing campaign

Initially, they might experience some success and excitement. Sales start coming in, validating their concept, and boosting their confidence. However, after a few months, they face several challenges:

- Sales decline unexpectedly
- Negative reviews start appearing due to shipping delays
- A competitor launches with lower prices
- Ad costs increase, squeezing profit margins

At this point, many entrepreneurs struggle. They are caught between the memory of initial success and the harsh reality of current challenges. This is where endurance becomes critical.

Common Pitfalls in This Scenario

- **Paralysis by analysis:** Overanalyzing the situation without acting.

- **Premature pivoting:** Abandoning the original idea too quickly without thorough evaluation.

- **Chasing vanity metrics:** Focusing on less important numbers (like social media followers) instead of core business metrics.

- **Neglecting customer feedback:** Not engaging with and learn from customer complaints and suggestions.

Endurance-Based Solutions

- **Data-driven problem-solving:** Analyze sales data, customer feedback, and market trends to find the root causes of declining performance.

- **Incremental improvements:** Focus on making small, continuous improvements rather than seeking a single, dramatic solution.
- **Customer engagement:** Proactively reach out to customers for feedback and work on improving their experience.
- **Supply chain optimization:** Negotiate with suppliers for better terms or find new suppliers to improve product quality and shipping times.
- **Differentiation Strategy:** Develop unique selling propositions that set the business apart from competitors, reducing reliance on price competition.

By applying these endurance-based approaches, the entrepreneur can weather the storm and position their baby business for sustainable growth.

Creating a Safe Environment for Growth

Your role as an entrepreneur is to create a safe environment for your baby business to thrive and learn. This means:

1. **Not placing unrealistic survival expectations on the business:**
Understand that growth takes time and rarely follows a smooth, predictable path.

2. Ensuring personal financial stability:

- Keep a day job or freelance work if possible
- Have sufficient savings to cover personal expenses for at least 6-12 months
- Consider part-time or flexible work arrangements that allow you to nurture your business

3. Being prepared to learn and adapt:

- Continually look for and act on customer feedback
- Stay informed about market trends and industry developments
- Be willing to pivot your business model if necessary

4. Creating a culture of experimentation:

- Encourage calculated risk-taking within the business
- View failures as learning opportunities rather than catastrophes

- Celebrate innovative thinking, even when ideas do not pan out

5. Building a supportive network:

- Connect with other entrepreneurs for mutual support and advice
- Seek mentors who have experience in your industry
- Join entrepreneur groups or co-working spaces to combat isolation

Remember, it is okay for a baby business to "fail forward." Each setback is an opportunity to learn and potentially pivot your business model if necessary.

The Power of the Minimum Viable Product (MVP)

One effective way to create a safe environment for your baby business is to adopt the Minimum Viable Product (MVP) approach:

1. Identify the core problem your business solves
2. Develop the simplest version of your product or service that addresses this problem

3. Launch this MVP to a small group of early adopters

4. Gather extensive feedback and usage data

5. Iterate and improve based on this real-world information

This approach allows you to test your business concept with minimal risk and investment, providing a safe space for your baby business to take its first steps.

The Trap of Future Success and How to Avoid It.

Many baby business owners get stuck in a mental loop, oscillating between dreams of future success and the harsh reality of present challenges. This trap can be particularly dangerous because it diverts energy and focus from the critical tasks of the present. It often manifests when entrepreneurs are caught in a cycle of envisioning their business's future triumphs while simultaneously grappling with the day-to-day struggles of running a startup.

Such confusion can lead to an emotional rollercoaster where every small success is seen through the lens of a future empire, and every setback feels like a personal failure against the backdrop of grand aspirations. This mindset can dangerously skew priorities, causing owners to neglect the foundational aspects of their business, such as customer service, product development, or financial management, in favor of chasing after what might be rather than what is.

To avoid this trap, business owners should adopt a balanced approach that integrates future planning with present action. This means setting clear, achievable short-term goals that contribute to the long-term vision while ensuring that the business still survives. Implementing practices like agile planning or other project management methods can help, where small, integrative steps are taken towards larger goals, allowing for flexibility and adjustment based on real-time feedback and results. Even just a simple kanban board can help to manage day-to-day and weekly tasks. But this will always depend on the type of baby business that you have or are about to start.

Moreover, mindfulness techniques can keep entrepreneurs grounded in the now, encouraging them to celebrate small victories and learn from the present challenges. By maintaining healthy focus on both the present and future, business owners can ensure they are grounded in the reality of building a business rather than dreaming about future success.

Signs You're Caught in the Future Success Trap.

- Spending more time dreaming about future achievements than working on current tasks
- Making decisions based on imagined future scenarios rather than present realities
- Neglecting immediate customer needs in favor of grandiose future plans
- Becoming discouraged when present-day results do not match your future vision

Strategies to Break Free from This Cycle

1. **Set realistic short-term goals:** Break down your long-term vision into **achievable** monthly or quarterly goals.

2. **Focus on leading indicators:** Pay attention to metrics that predict future success (e.g., customer engagement, retention rates) rather than just lagging indicators (e.g., revenue, profit).

3. **Implement regular reality checks:** Schedule weekly or monthly sessions to assess your progress objectively and realign your efforts with current realities.

4. **Practice mindfulness:** Use techniques like meditation to stay grounded in the present moment and reduce anxiety about the future.

5. **Celebrate small wins:** Acknowledge and appreciate incremental progress to maintain motivation and perspective.

Legendary business owners understand the power of being present. They focus on solving immediate problems rather than getting lost in projections of future revenues or profits.

Navigating Early Success: The Importance of Measured Optimism

Even when your baby business starts generating sales or gaining traction, it is important to maintain perspective:

1. **Don't get overly excited about initial wins:** Early success is encouraging but not a guarantee of long-term viability

2. **Avoid making premature decisions:** Resist the urge to rapidly expand or make large investments based on early positive signals.

3. **Analyze your success thoroughly:**

- Where are your sales or users coming from?
- Is your customer acquisition sustainable and repeatable?
- What's driving customer satisfaction and retention?

4. **Maintain operational discipline:** Continue to manage costs carefully and prioritize profitability over rapid growth.

5. **Plan for setbacks:** Use periods of success to build reserves (financial and otherwise) that can help you weather future challenges.

Case Study: The Dangers of Premature Scaling

Consider the story of a startup that developed a popular social media management tool:

- Month 1-3: Launched MVP, gained 1000 users through word-of-mouth
- Month 4: Featured on a major tech blog, user base grew to 10,000
- Month 5: Raised $500,000 in seed funding based on rapid growth
- Month 6: Hired a sales team and expanded office space
- Month 7: Growth slowed unexpectedly
- Month 8: Realized customer acquisition cost was unsustainable
- Month 9: Forced to lay off staff and downsize operations

The startup's mistake was assuming that early traction guaranteed continued rapid growth. By scaling prematurely, they increased their burn rate without a sustainable plan for continued user acquisition and retention.

The Role of Emotional Intelligence in Entrepreneurial Endurance.

Emotional intelligence (EQ) plays a crucial role in developing the endurance necessary for nurturing a baby business. High EQ enables entrepreneurs to:

1. **Manage stress effectively:** Recognize and mitigate the effects of stress before it becomes overwhelming.

2. **Communicate clearly:** Express ideas and concerns effectively to team members, investors, and customers.

3. **Build strong relationships:** Develop and maintain positive relationships with various stakeholders.

4. **Make balanced decisions:** Consider both emotional and logical factors when making critical business decisions.

5. **Demonstrate resilience:** Bounce back from setbacks and keep a positive outlook in the face of challenges.

Developing Emotional Intelligence

To enhance your emotional intelligence and build greater endurance:

1. **Practice self-awareness:** Regularly reflect on your emotions and their impact on your behavior and decision-making.

2. **Seek feedback:** Ask trusted colleagues, mentors, or friends for honest feedback about your emotional responses and interpersonal skills.

3. **Develop empathy:** Make a conscious effort to understand the perspectives and feelings of others, including customers, employees, and partners.

4. **Learn stress-management techniques:** Explore methods like deep breathing, progressive muscle relaxation, or mindfulness meditation to manage stress effectively.

5. **Continuously educate yourself:** Read books, attend workshops, or work with a coach to enhance your emotional intelligence skills.

Conclusion: The Equilibrium of Entrepreneurial Endurance

Enduring the challenges of a baby business is a game of emotional temperament and control. It requires finding a balance between:

- Optimism and realism
- Passion and detachment
- Vision and present-day focus
- Risk-taking and caution

Always remember:

- The future is an illusion for a baby business
- You do not have the luxury of extensive past data
- The only thing that is real is the present

Feel the present moment, endure its challenges, and keep moving forward. By maintaining this perspective and developing your endurance, you will be better equipped to nurture your baby business through its crucial stages of early growth.

Remember, entrepreneurship is a marathon, not a sprint. Your ability to endure the difficulties of raising your baby business will determine your long-term success. Embrace the journey, learn from every experience, and stay committed to your vision while staying flexible in your approach. With endurance, patience, and emotional intelligence, you can guide your baby business from its first tentative steps to confident strides in the marketplace.

Reflective Questions

1. *What specific challenges are currently testing your endurance as an entrepreneur? How are you coping with these challenges?*

2. *How can you build more resilience in both your business operations and your personal life? What practices or habits could you adopt?*

3. *Reflect on a time when you showed strong endurance in your business. What lessons can you draw from this experience?*

4. *What support systems do you currently have in place to help you endure tough times? How can you strengthen or expand these systems?*

5. *How do you manage the emotional rollercoaster of entrepreneurship? What strategies can you employ to maintain equilibrium?*

Chapter 6

Protecting Your Baby Business

The Delicate Balance of Nurturing and Protecting

Protecting your baby business is akin to protecting yourself, but it is crucial to recognize the distinction. As the founder, you are the nurturer and caregiver of your business. Without you, the business cannot survive at this early stage. However, it is vital to remember that while you can exist independently of the business, your business relies entirely on you for its existence.

This reality should provide you with a sense of perspective. When the lines between you and your business blur, you risk losing objectivity, potentially making decisions that protect your ego at the expense of the business's growth.

The Art of Handling Feedback: Distinguishing Valuable Input from Noise

Feedback is an essential part of business growth, but not all feedback is created equally. You will encounter diverse types of input:

- Constructive feedback from customers and stakeholders
- Criticism from skeptics and naysayers
- Well-intentioned but potentially misguided advice from friends and family

Developing the ability to discern valuable feedback from noise is crucial for your business's protection and growth. Here is how to approach this:

- **Establish feedback criteria**
    - Define what makes feedback valuable for your business

86

- o Include any relevant or specific sources of credulity
- o Take note of the actionable insights

- **Source evaluation**

  - o Consider the source's ability and their understanding of your business model
  - o Not all feedback should be weighted equally
  - o Prioritize sources of feedback with relevant experience or who are directly affected by your business operations
  - o Treat customer feedback as expertise – even if this seems counterintuitive
  - o Remember that the message is still more important than the messenger

- **Pattern recognition**

  - o Look for recurring themes in the feedback
  - o If multiple sources independently mention the same issue or opportunity, there is a higher chance it calls for attention

- o Use identified patterns to make informed decisions

- **Feedback filtering**
  - o Use tools or systems to categorize feedback
  - o Customer feedback software can help segregate genuine customer reviews from spam or biased comments

- **Feedback implementation**
  - o When deciding to act on feedback you should consider the potential impact on your business
  - o Smaller, low-risk changes can often be tested quickly
  - o Larger pivots or changes will require more careful consideration

- **Emotional detachment**
  - o Learn to separate your emotional response from the feedback
  - o Objectively evaluate criticism without feeling personally attacked or overly

influenced   by   praise

- **Continuous learning**
  - Treat feedback as a learning opportunity
  - Even if the feedback is not what you want to hear it can provide valuable lessons or perspectives you have not yet considered

- **Feedback loop**
  - Create mechanisms to acknowledge and sometimes act on feedback
  - Inform those who provided feedback of changes made or reasons for not making changes
  - This improves your product or service by building trust and engagement with your customer base

Dealing with Skepticism

Many individuals will project their insecurities onto your venture. They might question your ideas, doubt your capabilities, or predict failure based on others' experiences. Remember, these reactions often stem from their own limitations. To protect your business:

- Develop resilience against unfounded criticism
- Learn to filter out unconstructive noise
- Stay focused on your vision and goals

Embracing Constructive Feedback

While it is important to filter out negativity, be careful not to dismiss all criticism. Constructive feedback is essential for growth and improvement. For example: Imagine you launch a home-based beverage business. Customers praise the taste but mention that the part sizes are small. Instead of defensively ignoring this feedback, consider it an opportunity for improvement. You could explore options like offering larger sizes or adjusting your pricing strategy.

Balancing Personal Ego and Business Needs

Your initial protective instinct might be to shield your ego, but this can be detrimental to your business. To truly protect your baby business:

- Listen to feedback objectively
- Evaluate criticism without personal bias

- Implement changes that help your business, even if they challenge your initial ideas.

Navigating the Spectrum of Opinions

It is important to note that not all feedback should be treated equally. You will meet individuals who may cite past failures of similar businesses. However, remember that those other ventures did not have you at the helm. Several factors could have contributed to their failure - regulatory issues, supply chain problems, or market conditions that may not apply to your situation.

The journey of a business often follows a pattern:

- Initial skepticism from others
- Criticism and doubt
- Potential ridicule
- Accusations of being unrealistic
- Either recognition of success or learning from failure.

Even in the case of failure, it is not the end of the road. You learn, recover, and try again. This is the reality of business - failures occur, but they do not define the end of your entrepreneurial journey.

The key is making sure you do not let external noises box you into a defensive position. Avoid getting so caught up in defending yourself that you neglect to protect and improve your business. That is a common pitfall that can be avoided with the right mindset.

Creating a Nurturing Environment for Your Business

Protecting your baby business is not just about handling feedback. It is about creating an environment where it can thrive. This often requires making some challenging decisions.

The Employment Dilemma

If keeping your current employment is necessary to fund your living expenses, it is advisable to do so. Avoid leaving your stable job prematurely when your business is still in its infancy. Unless you have 6-12 months of expenses saved - consider it akin to taking an extended leave to care for your business - keeping your job can provide crucial stability.

Without this financial cushion, you risk putting yourself in a precarious position. Financial stress can impair your decision-making abilities, potentially harming both you and your business. This is not a cinematic scenario; it is real life. Approach your venture with strategic thinking and financial prudence.

The Knowledge Acquisition Game

If you are venturing into an established field - such as retail or service industries - you face a unique set of challenges. It is essential to delve deep into various aspects of business management:

- Financial planning and forecasting
- Regulatory compliance and documentation
- Accounting and bookkeeping
- Cash flow management
- Planning and operations
- Inventory control
- Supply chain optimization

There are primarily two routes to acquiring this knowledge:

- Engage in extensive research and learning as you go
- Partner with or seek mentorship from experienced individuals in your field.

- Whichever path you choose, it is crucial to cultivate a thirst for knowledge. Continuous learning is key. Without equipping yourself with these tools, you risk entering a competitive market underprepared.

The Art of Strategic Planning for a Baby Business (Based on Existing Models)

When protecting your baby business that is based on an existing business model - like a restaurant, laundromat, convenience store, or similar established ventures - your strategic planning takes on a different flavor. You are not reinventing the wheel, but you still need to roll it effectively. Here is how to approach it:

1. Study the Existing Playbook

For businesses with established models, there is often a wealth of information available. Your job is to become a student of the industry:

- Research successful businesses in your chosen field
- Understand the standard operating procedures in your industry
- Identify the typical challenges and how successful businesses overcome them

For example, if you are opening a laundromat:

- Study the typical equipment needs and costs
- Understand peak usage times and how to manage them
- Learn about water and energy efficiency practices in the industry

2. Localize Your Strategy

While the overall business model may be established, your local market is unique:

- Conduct demographic research in your area
- Understand local regulations and requirements specific to your business type
- Identify gaps in the local market that your business could fill

For a restaurant, this might mean:

- Analyzing the local dining scene to find underserved cuisines or styles
- Understanding local food sourcing options and costs
- Researching local dining habits and preferences

3. Financial Planning with Benchmarks

Use industry standards as a starting point for your financial planning:

- Research average startup costs for your type of business
- Understand typical profit margins in your industry

- Use industry benchmarks for expenses like rent, labor, and inventory

For a convenience store, you might:

- Study typical inventory turnover rates
- Understand standard markup practices in the industry
- Research average daily sales for similar stores in comparable locations

4. Operational Excellence Through Established Best Practices

Learn from what works in your chosen industry:

- Study standard operating procedures for your business type
- Understand typical staffing needs and structures
- Learn about common technology and tools used in your industry

In a laundromat business, this could involve:

97

- Understanding the best layout for machines to maximize space and customer flow
- Learning about maintenance schedules for laundry equipment
- Researching popular payment systems used in modern laundromats

5. Marketing with a Twist

While you are entering an established market, you are marketing still needs to stand out:

- Understand typical marketing strategies in your industry
- Look for ways to differentiate your business within the established framework
- Learn from both successful and unsuccessful marketing campaigns in your field

For a restaurant, consider:

- Studying how successful local restaurants use social media

- Understanding what type of promotions work well in your area
- Learning about loyalty programs that have been effective in similar establishments

6. Risk Management Based on Known Challenges

Every established business model has known risks. Your job is to prepare for them:

- Research common pitfalls in your chosen industry
- Understand typical insurance needs for your business type
- Learn about standard safety and security measures

For a convenience store, this might include:
- Understanding how to prevent and handle shoplifting
- Learning about cash management and security best practices

- Studying food safety regulations and how to comply with them

7. Networking and Learning from Established Players

In established industries, there is often a wealth of experience you can tap into:

- Join industry associations relevant to your business
- Attend trade shows and conferences in your field
- Consider finding a mentor who has success in your chosen business model

For any of these businesses - be it a laundromat, restaurant, or convenience store - connecting with successful owners in non-competing markets can offer invaluable insights.

The Mindset of a Business Protector

Protecting your baby business requires more than just tactics; it is a mindset. Consider the following principles:

1. **Continuous Learning:** Absorb knowledge from various sources. Stay informed about your industry and business management practices.

2. **Maintain Your Drive:** Keep your entrepreneurial spirit alive. Complacency can be a significant threat to your business.

3. **Adaptability:** Be prepared to adjust your strategies as market conditions change. Flexibility is key to long-term success.

4. **Data-Driven Decision Making:** While intuition has its place, back up your decisions with solid data and analysis.

5. **Balanced Perspective:** Keep a long-term vision while focusing on short-term goals and milestones.

The Reality of Business Protection

It is important to acknowledge that protecting your baby business is a challenging endeavor. It will test your resolve and capabilities in unprecedented ways. There will be moments of doubt and difficulty.

However, it is crucial to remember your first motivation. Recall the passion and vision that inspired you to start this journey. This foundational drive will be your anchor during challenging times.

Remember, you are not just building a business; you are creating a potential legacy. You are solving problems, creating value, that will make an impact. That is worth protecting and nurturing.

Conclusion: Protect your Baby, not yourself

Ultimately, protecting your baby business comes down to this: Be strategic, be adaptable, and maintain your vision. Filter out unproductive noise but remain open to constructive input. Create an environment where your business can flourish, even if it requires personal sacrifices.

When starting a baby business based on an existing model, you are not trying to reinvent the industry. Your goal is to understand the established playbook thoroughly and then execute it effectively in your specific context. This approach allows you to benefit from proven strategies while still finding ways to make your business unique and competitive in your local market.

As the guardian of your baby business, it is your responsibility to nurture it, protect it, and help its growth. Approach this task with determination, objectivity, and a willingness to learn and adapt. When you protect your baby business effectively, you are not just securing your own future - you are paving the way for potentially significant achievements.

Your baby business depends on your guidance and protection. Embrace this responsibility with the seriousness and dedication it deserves, and you will be well-positioned to navigate the challenges of entrepreneurship.

Reflective Questions

1. *What are the most significant potential threats or risks your business is currently facing? How can you proactively address these?*

2. *How do you currently differentiate between constructive feedback and unhelpful criticism? What criteria do you use, and how can you refine this process?*

3. *In what ways might you be overprotecting your business, potentially hindering its growth? How can you find a better balance?*

4. *What steps can you take to create a more nurturing environment for your business while still allowing it room to grow and learn from mistakes?*

5. *What is a safe way to protect your business's core values and mission as it grows and faces new challenges?*

Chapter 7

The Baby Business Has Survived: Navigating the Next Phase

The Milestone of Survival

Your baby business has survived. Take a moment to appreciate this achievement. It is no small feat. But now, you are standing at a crossroads, and the real work begins. This is where you start asking yourself the tough questions: Can this business sustain my fundamental lifestyle while I dive in full-time to develop it further into something great?

It is time to get real with yourself. This is not the time for rose-colored glasses or wishful thinking.

Measuring Survival: The Metrics That Matter

First things first, you need to understand what "survival" really means for your business. It is not just about having a pulse; it is about showing signs of real life. Here is what you need to be looking at:

- Cash Flow: Is your business generating revenue consistently? More importantly, is it not burning through cash like a California wildfire?
- Basic Expenses: Can you cover the essentials? We are talking rent, utilities, supplies - the bare bones of keeping your business operational.
- Personal Salary: Are you able to pay yourself anything? Even if it is just enough to buy ramen noodles, it is a start.
- Customer Data: Have you built up a solid base of information about your customers? This is not just names and numbers; it is about understanding their needs, behaviors, and feedback.
- Growth Potential: Are you at a point where you are considering hiring your first employee? That is a big step, and it is a clear sign that your baby business is ready to start walking.

Remember, these benchmarks are personal. What works for one business might not work for another. When I was running TheChumEffect (TCE), I had the luxury of staying at my brother's place rent-free for two years. That was my lifeline. You might not have that, and that is okay. Your path is your own.

The Reality Check: Movie Magic vs. Real Life

Let us bust a myth right now. You know those movies where the passionate entrepreneur quits their cushy job, throws caution to the wind, and dives headfirst into their dream business? Yeah, that's Hollywood BS for the most part.

In the real world, you need a support system. Whether it is friends, family, savings, or a day job that pays the bills, you need something to fall back on. Trying to raise a baby business without resources is like trying to raise a real baby without a roof over your head or food in the fridge. It is not just tough; it is nearly impossible.

When TCE finally hit its stride, it did not happen overnight. I started with a measly $50 profit from one client. But that $50 was everything. It was proof of concept, a glimmer of what could be. From there, it grew - slowly but surely - until it could cover my living expenses. Only then did I make the leap to my own place.

Transitioning from Baby to Toddler: A Detailed Guide

As your baby business starts to find its footing, you will feel the shift. It is like watching a child take their first steps - exciting, nerve-wracking, and full of potential tumbles. Here is how to navigate this crucial transition:

Recognizing the Signs

Your business is ready for its toddler phase when:
- You have a consistent customer base
- Revenue is stable (even if not huge)
- You are starting to think beyond day-to-day survival

Structural Changes

- **Formalizing Processes:**

  o   Document your workflows

- o Create standard operating procedures
- o Implement basic quality control measures

- **Financial Management:**

  - o Move beyond basic bookkeeping
  - o Start forecasting and budgeting
  - o Consider hiring a part-time accountant or financial advisor

- **Team Building:**

  - o Find key roles you need to fill
  - o Start with part-time or contract help before full-time hires
  - o Develop a basic onboarding process

Strategic Shifts

- **From Reactive to Proactive:**

  - o Start planning quarters ahead, not just weeks

- o   Anticipate market changes and customer needs
- o   Develop a basic risk management strategy

- **Customer Relationship Management:**

  - o   Implement a CRM system, even a simple one
  - o   Focus on customer retention, not just acquisition
  - o   Start gathering and acting on customer feedback systematically

- **Marketing Evolution:**
  - o   Move beyond word-of-mouth and personal networks
  - o   Develop a consistent brand voice and image
  - o   Experiment with different marketing channels

Mindset Adjustments

- **Delegation:**

- o Learn to let go of some control
- o Trust your team (even if it is just one or two people)
- o Focus on what you do best, outsource the rest

- **Strategic Thinking:**
  - o Set aside time for planning and strategy
  - o Start thinking about long-term goals
  - o Consider potential pivots or expansions
  - **Personal Growth:**
    - o Invest in your own learning and development
    - o Network with other business owners at a similar stage
    - o Consider finding a mentor or coach.

Remember, this transition is not about sudden, dramatic changes. It is a gradual process of building on your foundation, much like a toddler does not suddenly start running marathons. Take it step by step, celebrate the small victories, and do not be afraid to stumble. That is how your business learns to walk.

Conclusion: Embracing the Journey

Your baby business has survived, and now the real adventure begins. This is where you start to see the fruits of your labor, but it is also where the stakes get higher. Stay focused, stay hungry, but also stay grounded.

Remember why you started this journey in the first place. Keep that fire burning but temper it with the wisdom you have gained. Your business is not just surviving anymore - it is ready to thrive.

Are you ready for the next phase? Because ready or not, it is here. Buckle up, keep learning, and enjoy the ride. This is what you have been working for. Now make it count.

Reflective Questions

1. *What specific metrics or milestones show that your business has moved beyond mere survival? How are you tracking these?*

2. *How are you preparing your business operations and mindset for the next phase*

of growth? What specific changes are you implementing?

3. *What new challenges do you expect as your business transitions from infancy to toddlerhood? How can you proactively prepare for these?*

4. *In what ways might you need to adjust your leadership style as your business grows? What new skills do you need to develop?*

5. *How can you keep the agility and innovation of a baby business while implementing the structures needed for growth?*

Chapter 8

Your Business is Your Baby: Embracing the Journey

The Essence of Your Baby Business

Throughout this book, we have explored the concept of your business as a baby. Now, it is time to drive home to this point. Your business is not just a project or a venture - it is your baby. It is a living, breathing entity that you have nurtured from conception to its current state.

Remember when Mark Zuckerberg famously rejected offers to sell Facebook? He said he could not sell his baby. People thought he was crazy at the time but look where that decision led. He understood something fundamental that many entrepreneurs forget: a baby business is exactly that - a baby.

The Danger of False Comparisons

Here is where many entrepreneurs go wrong: they start comparing their baby business to the adults in the room. Let us get one thing straight - you are not Meta, Amazon, Tesla, Google, or any of the banking giants. Not yet. And that is okay.

These companies are playing in a different league altogether. They have:
- Billions in resources
- Massive teams of experts
- Years (sometimes decades) of market experience
- Established brand recognition
- The ability to influence entire markets.

You, on the other hand, are still learning to walk. And that is exactly where you should be.

Staying Grounded in Reality.

The key to success in the early stages of your business is to stay grounded. This means:

- **Recognizing Your Stage:** Understand where you are in your business journey. Embrace being a baby business.

- **Making Appropriate Decisions:** Your decisions should be focused on survival and gradual growth, not on competing with industry giants.

- **Setting Realistic Goals:** Do not aim for world domination just yet. Focus on achievable, incremental goals.

- **Learning Continuously:** Every experience, whether success or failure, is a learning opportunity. Absorb these lessons.

- **Celebrating Small Wins:** In the baby stage, every little achievement is significant. Recognize and celebrate these milestones.

The Power of Introspection

Personal experience has taught me the value of introspective reflection. My journey with the Chumz business was a profound learning experience. It was through deep, honest self-reflection that I truly began to understand what the game of business was all about.

This process of introspection can help you:
- Identify your strengths and weaknesses
- Understand your true motivations
- Recognize patterns in your decision-making
- Develop a clearer vision for your business's future

Lessons from the Trenches

Here are some key lessons I have learned that might help you on your journey:
- **Patience is Crucial:** Growth takes time. Do not rush the process.
- **Flexibility is Key:** Be ready to pivot when necessary. The ability to adapt is often what separates successful businesses from failed ones.

- **Focus on Value Creation:** Always ask yourself, "How is my business adding value to my customers' lives?"

- **Build Strong Foundations:** In the early stages, focus on building robust systems and processes. These will support your growth later.

- **Nurture Relationships:** Your network can be your net worth. Build genuine relationships in your industry.

- **Trust Your Instincts, But Verify:** While gut feelings are important, always back them up with data and research.

The Journey Ahead

As you continue your entrepreneurial journey, remember that every big business started as someone's baby. Apple was once just two guys in a garage.

Amazon started as an online bookstore. Google began as a research project.

Your business has the potential to grow into something amazing. But for now, it needs your care, attention, and protection. Nurture it. Guide it. Let it stumble and learn. And most importantly, give it time to grow.

Conclusion: Embrace Your Baby Business

In conclusion, embrace your status as a baby business. Do not be in a rush to grow up too fast. Each stage of business growth comes with its own challenges and rewards. By fully experiencing and learning from the baby stage, you are laying the groundwork for future success.

Remember, your business is unique. Its journey will be unlike any other. Stay true to your vision, learn from your experiences, and keep moving forward. The road ahead may be challenging, but it is also incredibly rewarding.

Your business is your baby. Love it, nurture it, and watch it grow into something truly remarkable.

Reflective Questions

1. *How can you keep a long-term perspective while still focusing on day-to-day operations? What practices can help you balance these two perspectives?*

2. *In what specific ways can you show more care and nurturing to your business? How might this impact its growth and success?*

3. *What personal habits or mindsets do you need to adjust to better serve your growing business? How can you go about making these changes?*

4. *How do you embrace the unique journey of your business instead of comparing it to others? What metrics or benchmarks would be more appropriate for your specific situation?*

5. *Reflect on your entrepreneurial journey so far. What are the most valuable lessons you have learned, and how can you apply these moving forward?*

Chapter 9

Snippet into Business as a Toddler: Guidance, Growth, and Grit

Welcome to the Toddler Years

Congratulations, your business has graduated from babyhood. You are now in the toddler phase, and let me tell you, it is a wild ride. Just like a real-life toddler, your business is going to be all over the place. One day you are on top of the world, the next you are face-planting into the sandbox. But that is okay – it is all part of the process.

The Critical Role of Mentorship and Guidance

This is where things get real. You need the right mentorship and guidance like a toddler needs a patient parent. It is time to:

- Sign up for incubators
- Join accelerator programs
- Seek out mentorship opportunities

But here is the kicker: not all advice is good advice. Choose caution here because you might get inaccurate information that can lead down a path which is great for someone else's business, but disastrous for yours. You will need to be very discerning with information and practice introspective reflection.

The Art of Asking Questions

You must be curious. Constantly. Ask questions until you understand, and then ask some more. Do not just do things because some guru or well-meaning advisor tells you to. Understand the 'why' behind every action.

Always ask yourself: "Does this apply to my business right now?"

For example, let us talk about hiring. Everyone might be telling you it is time to expand your team. But ask yourself:

- Am I really at capacity?
- Can I handle things on my own for a bit longer?
- What specific skills am I missing that I cannot develop myself?
- Will hiring now propel my business forward or drain my resources?

Remember, just because others are doing something does not mean it is right for you. Your business is unique, and so is its growth trajectory.

The Balancing Act

The toddler phase is all about balance. You are learning to:

- Negotiate: With suppliers, potential partners, even your first big clients.
- Form alliances: Network with other businesses, join industry groups.
- Navigate conflicts: Not everyone will be your friend in business.

This is where you will form relationships that can help or hinder you in your teenage and adult business years. Choose wisely because some of these connections will grow alongside you.

Embracing the Battle Scars

Get ready for your first real business battle scars. They might sting, but they are valuable. You might experience:

- Losses on deals you thought were a sure thing
- Early clients jumping ship
- Products or services that flop

But here is the thing: each of these experiences teaches you something crucial. You are learning how the game is really played. And with each setback, you are getting tougher, smarter, and more prepared for the next challenge.

The Toddler Mindset

Developing the right mindset during this phase is crucial. Here is what you need to cultivate:

- Resilience: You are going to fall. A lot. The key is getting back up every single time.
- Adaptability: The market will throw curveballs. Be ready to pivot.
- Curiosity: Never stop learning. Your industry is evolving, and so should you.
- Confidence: Trust your instincts but verify with data.
- Humility: Know when to ask for help. No one builds a successful business entirely on their own.

Making Informed Decisions

As a toddler business, you are going to face a lot of decisions. Some will be easy; others will keep you up at night. Here is how to approach them:

- Gather Information: Do not make decisions in a vacuum. Research, ask for advice, look at case studies.
- Analyze the Impact: How will this decision affect your business in the short and long term?
- Trust Your Gut: Sometimes, after you have done all the analysis, you need to trust your instincts.
- Learn from the Outcome: Whether the decision turns out good or bad, there is always a lesson to be learned.

The Power of Community

Remember, you are not on this journey alone. There are other toddler businesses out there, stumbling and growing just like you. Connecting with them can be invaluable:

- Join entrepreneur groups

- Attend industry meetups
- Take part in online forums
- Collaborate on projects

These connections can provide support, inspiration, and sometimes even lead to business opportunities.

Preparing for the Next Phase

As you navigate the toddler years, keep your eyes on the horizon. The teenage years of your business are coming, and they bring their own set of challenges and opportunities. Use this time to:

- Build a strong foundation
- Develop robust systems and processes
- Cultivate a distinct brand identity
- Understand your market inside and out

Conclusion: Embrace the Chaos

The toddler phase of your business is chaotic, challenging, and crucial. It is where you will make mistakes, learn hard lessons, and start to see the real potential of what you are building. Embrace it all – the ups, the downs, the skinned knees, and the small victories.

Remember, every successful business you admire went through this phase. They stumbled, they fell, they got back up, and they kept moving forward. That is exactly what you are going to do.

You have survived the baby phase. You are learning to walk, talk, and make your mark on the world. Now it is time to run, fall, get back up, and run again. You are not just ready to kick ass – you are already doing it. Keep going. The best is yet to come.

Reflective Questions

1. *What specific types of mentorships or guidance does your business need at this stage? How can you go about securing this support?*

2. *How are you currently balancing the need for structure with the need for flexibility in your business? Where might you need to adjust?*

3. *What new skills do you need to develop as your business grows? How do you plan to get these skills?*

4. *How can you create a culture of continuous learning and adaptation in your growing business? What specific practices or policies could support this?*

5. *As your business enters its "toddler" phase, how can you keep the entrepreneurial spirit and innovation that drove its early success?*

Coming Soon: The Complete "Business as a Baby" Series

Thank you for reading "Business as a Baby". Your entrepreneurial journey is just beginning, and we are excited to continue growing with you. This book is the first in a four-part series that will guide you through the entire lifecycle of your business. Here is what you can look forward to:

Business as a Toddler

Just as your business finds its footing, new challenges arise. Learn how to:

- Navigate the "terrible twos" of business growth
- Build and manage your first team
- Establish systems and processes for scalability
- Develop a strong brand identity.

Business as a Teenager

As your business matures, it faces complex decisions and opportunities. Discover how to:

- Manage rapid growth and expansion
- Handle increased competition
- Develop leadership skills for a growing organization
- Balance innovation with stability.

Business as an Adult

In the final stage, your business reaches maturity. Explore strategies for:

- Maintaining market leadership
- Diversifying product lines or entering new markets

- Preparing for potential exit strategies or succession planning
- Leaving a legacy in your industry

Each book in the series builds upon the lessons of the earlier one, providing you with a comprehensive guide to growing and sustaining your business through every stage of its development.

Stay tuned for the release of ***"Business as a Toddler"***, coming soon!

Author Biography.

The Journey from Setback to Universal Innovation:
Meet Chukwudum "Chumze" Chukwudebelu

When Chukwudum "Chumze" Chukwudebelu's first business venture failed, he didn't just learn from his mistakes—he uncovered a universal truth about business development that would transform how entrepreneurs and organizations of all sizes approach new ventures. His journey from failure to breakthrough innovation offers invaluable lessons for anyone involved in building or growing a business.

After moving from Nigeria to further his education in the United States, Chumze discovered his entrepreneurial spark through an unexpected avenue: college textbooks. What began as a successful textbook arbitrage business, generating $2,000 in weekly revenue during his college years, led to an ambitious vision for a textbook exchange app. However, this startup would teach him his most valuable lesson—one that would resonate with entrepreneurs and business leaders worldwide.

The critical insight came when Chumze realized he had approached his startup like an established corporation rather than the fledgling venture it was. This epiphany led to the development of the groundbreaking Business as a Baby (BAAB) framework. This innovative approach identifies four distinct developmental stages that every business must navigate:

- Baby: The crucial survival stage where fundamentals are established
- Toddler: The experimental phase of Mentorship, Guidance and Early Growth.
- Teenager: The rapid growth and scaling and product Market-fit Phase
- Adult: The maturity phase of established market presence

Through his framework, Chumze demonstrates that just as we wouldn't expect a child to run before walking, we shouldn't expect any new venture—whether from a solo entrepreneur or a Fortune 500 company—to run like a mature business.

As founder of TheChumEffect (TCE), Chumze has transformed these insights into actionable guidance for a diverse range of clients. His consulting firm helps everyone from first-time entrepreneurs to seasoned business leaders understand a fundamental truth: every new venture, regardless of its backing or origin, starts as a baby. This principle has proven invaluable for:

- Independent entrepreneurs starting their first venture
- Established companies launching new divisions or products
- Consulting firms guiding clients through different growth stages
- Small business owners expanding into new markets
- Innovation teams within organizations
- Anyone embarking on a new business venture

"Business as a Baby," the first book in a planned four-part series, focuses specifically on the critical baby stage—the make-or-break period where survival is the only goal that matters. Through its pages, Chumze shares not just strategies and frameworks, but a fundamentally new way of thinking about the earliest stage of business development. He details why this stage requires unique approaches to:

- Resource allocation
- Decision-making
- Growth expectations
- Risk management
- Market approach
- Team building

Today, Chumze continues to guide entrepreneurs and organizations through their growth journeys, helping them avoid the pitfalls he once encountered and embrace the natural stages of business development. His story serves as both inspiration and warning: inspiration that failure can lead to revolutionary insights, and warning that even the most promising ventures—whether backed by substantial resources or bootstrap funding—can stumble if they try to run before, they can walk.

In "Business as a Baby," Chumze offers readers more than just business advice—he provides a proven framework for nurturing ventures through their most vulnerable stage. His work demonstrates that whether you're starting your first business in your garage or launching a new division within an established company, understanding and respecting the baby stage is essential for building a foundation for future growth.

For anyone involved in building or growing a business venture, Chumze's insights offer invaluable guidance on how to navigate the critical baby phase. His message transcends the scale and scope of business: understanding and respecting your venture's developmental stage isn't just helpful—it's essential for survival and growth in today's competitive marketplace.

Through his work with TheChumEffect and now through "Business as a Baby" Chumze isn't just sharing his personal story of transformation—he's providing a universal framework that helps everyone from solo entrepreneurs to corporate innovators build sustainable, successful businesses. His insights have proven that whether you're starting small or launching with substantial resources, the principles of nurturing a business through its baby stage remain fundamentally the same.

Look for the upcoming books in the series— **"Business as a Toddler,"** **"Business as a Teenager,"** and **"Business as an Adult"**—which will complete

Chumze's comprehensive guide to business growth and development through all four crucial stages.

Made in the USA
Columbia, SC
21 February 2025

54187402R00076